THE LEGEND OF THE BERMUDA TRIANGLE

by **Thomas Kingsley Troupe**   illustrated by **Carlos Aon**

PICTURE WINDOW BOOKS
a capstone imprint

Thanks to our advisers for their expertise, research, and advice:

Elizabeth Tucker, Professor of English
Binghamton University
Binghamton, New York

Terry Flaherty, PhD, Professor of English
Minnesota State University, Mankato

Editor: Jennifer Besel
Designer: Nathan Gassman
Production Specialist: Jane Klenk
The illustrations in this book were created digitally.

Picture Window Books
151 Good Counsel Drive
P.O. Box 669
Mankato, MN 56002-0669
877-845-8392
www.capstonepub.com

Printed in the United States of America in North Mankato, Minnesota.
112010
006017R

All books published by Picture Window Books
are manufactured with paper containing at least
10 percent post-consumer waste.

Library of Congress Cataloging-in-Publication Data
Troupe, Thomas Kingsley.
The legend of the Bermuda Triangle / by Thomas Kingsley
Troupe ; illustrated by Carlos Aon.
p. cm.—(Legend has it)
Includes bibliographical references and index.
Summary: "Describes the legend of the Bermuda Triangle,
including how it started and what the legend says about the
place"—Provided by publisher.
ISBN 978-1-4048-6034-6 (lib. bdg.)
1. Bermuda Triangle—Juvenile literature. I. Title.
II. Series.
G558.T76 2011
001.94—dc22   2009050168

TABLE of CONTENTS

An OCEAN of MYSTERY

A ship cuts through the ocean waves.

Suddenly, it disappears.

It's lost in the
Bermuda Triangle!

The legend of the Bermuda Triangle started more than 50 years ago. Many believe the Triangle is a place where planes, boats, and people vanish.

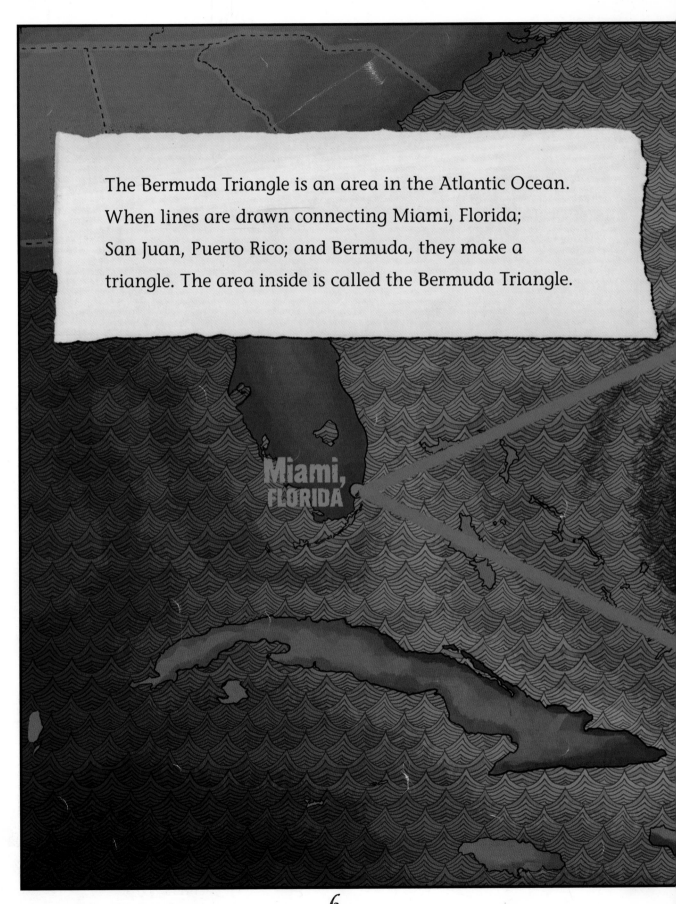

The Bermuda Triangle is an area in the Atlantic Ocean. When lines are drawn connecting Miami, Florida; San Juan, Puerto Rico; and Bermuda, they make a triangle. The area inside is called the Bermuda Triangle.

Miami, FLORIDA

Bermuda

San Juan,
PUERTO RICO

MYSTERIOUS DISAPPEARANCES

The legend of Flight 19 is the most famous Triangle story. In 1945, five planes left Florida on a training flight. Soon the pilots were lost and called for help. Stories say the lost pilots were heard over the radio, saying the water looked green instead of white like it usually did.

The U.S. Navy sent a seaplane to find the lost aircraft. That seaplane, along with the other five planes, disappeared. No wreckage from Flight 19 or the seaplane was found.

As she turned to go home, Cascio and her plane **vanished.**

As Triangle stories spread, people searched old records for information about other disappearances. Some blamed the Bermuda Triangle for the vanishings.

In 1921, a ship called the *Carroll A. Deering* had been found off the coast of North Carolina.

The crew was gone.

Were they lost as the ship sailed through the Triangle?

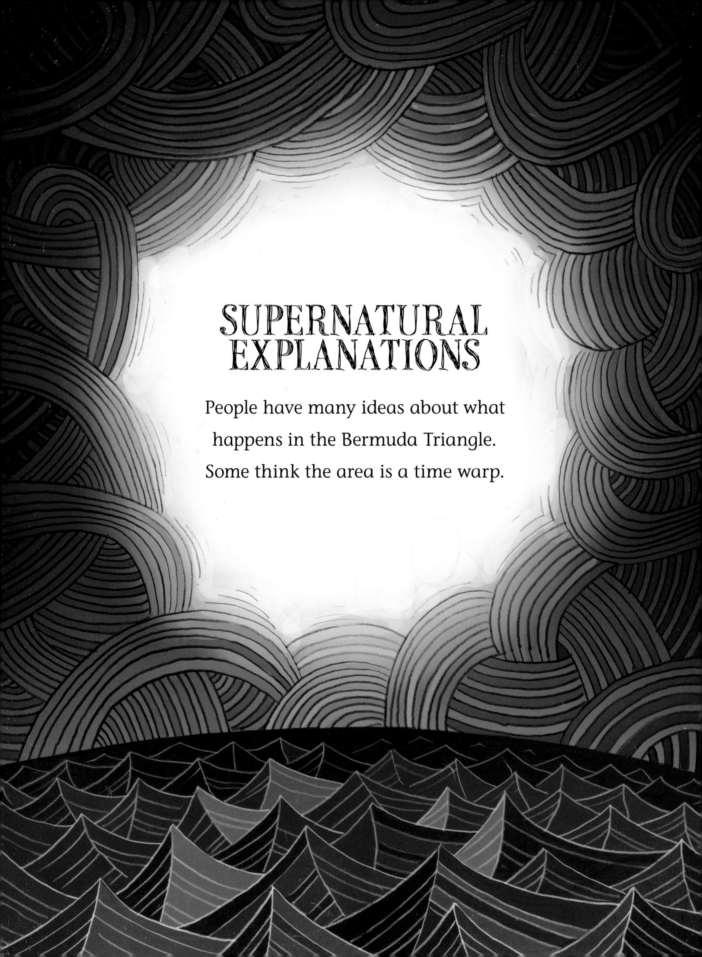

SUPERNATURAL EXPLANATIONS

People have many ideas about what happens in the Bermuda Triangle. Some think the area is a time warp.

Another idea is that space aliens took the vehicles. Some people claim to see strange lights above the Bermuda Triangle.

Are those lights spaceships?

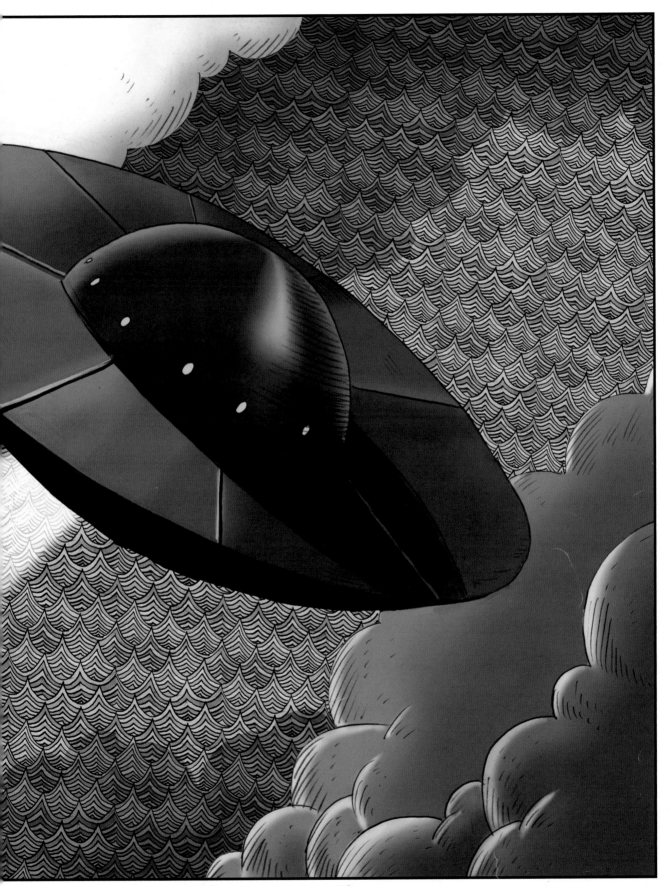

Other people believe the Bermuda Triangle is connected to another legend. They say a huge island called Atlantis lies inside the Bermuda Triangle. According to legend, the island sank thousands of years ago. But old weapons from the island shoot planes and boats.

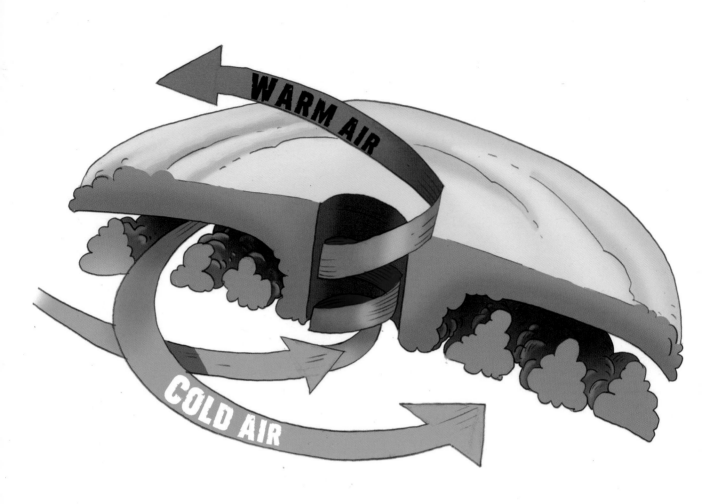

SCIENTIFIC EXPLANATIONS

Some researchers think science explains the mystery.
Warm and cold air mix at the Bermuda Triangle.
Strong winds and waves can appear quickly. These
storms may destroy planes and ships.

Some experts think the Bermuda Triangle has a strong magnetic field. The field can make compasses spin wildly and make equipment stop working. Even Christopher Columbus said his compass acted strangely while in the Sargasso Sea, near the Bermuda Triangle.

Without working equipment, pilots and sailors would be lost at sea.

Other scientists believe the Gulf Stream carries boats off course. The Gulf Stream is an ocean current that flows through the Bermuda Triangle. The current is strong and could push boats far out to sea.

The Gulf Stream doesn't affect airplane flight.
But the current could carry off a plane that crashes
in the Bermuda Triangle.

The Bermuda Triangle Today

More than 100 ships and planes have vanished in the Bermuda Triangle. But many others have traveled unharmed through the area.

What happens in the Bermuda Triangle?

We may never know.

GLOSSARY

compass—an instrument used for finding directions; a compass has a magnetic needle that always points north

crew—a team of people who work together on a ship, an aircraft, or a specific job

current—moving water that flows faster than the rest of the water

legend—a story handed down from earlier times that could seem believable

magnetic field—an area of moving electrical currents that affects other objects

time warp—a place where something from one time is moved to another time in the past or future; time warps have not been proven to exist

vanish—to disappear suddenly

READ MORE

Belanger, Jeff. *The Mysteries of the Bermuda Triangle.* New York: Grosset & Dunlap, 2010.

Hamilton, Sue. *The Bermuda Triangle.* Unsolved Mysteries. Edina, Minn.: Abdo Pub., 2008.

Walker, Kathyrn. *Mysteries of the Bermuda Triangle.* Unsolved! New York: Crabtree Pub., 2009.

INTERNET SITES

FactHound offers a safe, fun way to find Internet sites related to this book. All of the sites on FactHound have been researched by our staff.

Here's all you do:

Visit *www.facthound.com*

FactHound will fetch the best sites for you!

INDEX

LEGEND HAS IT
OTHER TITLES

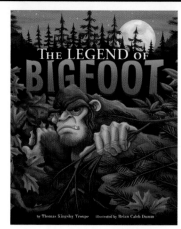

The Legend of Bigfoot

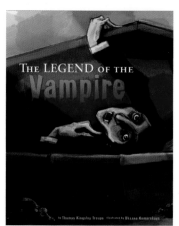

The Legend of the Vampire

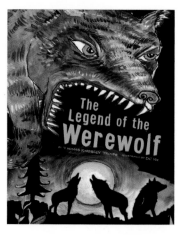

The Legend of the Werewolf